First World War
and Army of Occupation
War Diary
France, Belgium and Germany

51 DIVISION
154 Infantry Brigade
Loyal North Lancashire Regiment
1/4th Battalion (Territorial Force)
22 October 1914 - 31 December 1915

WO95/2887/4

The Naval & Military Press Ltd
www.nmarchive.com
Published in association with The National Archives

Published by

The Naval & Military Press Ltd

Unit 10 Ridgewood Industrial Park,

Uckfield, East Sussex,

TN22 5QE England

Tel: +44 (0) 1825 749494

www.naval-military-press.com

www.nmarchive.com

This diary has been reprinted in facsimile from the original. Any imperfections are inevitably reproduced and the quality may fall short of modern type and cartographic standards.

© **Crown Copyright**
Images reproduced by permission of The National Archives, London, England, 2015.

Contents

Document type	Place/Title	Date From	Date To
Heading	WO95/2887/4 1/4 Battalion Loyal North Lancashire Regiment		
Heading	51st Division 154th Infy Bde 1-4th Bn Loy Nth Lancs 1915 May-Dec 1915		
War Diary	Bedford	02/05/1915	02/05/1915
War Diary	Southampton	02/05/1915	02/05/1915
War Diary	Havre	02/05/1915	03/05/1915
War Diary	Bedford	03/05/1915	04/05/1915
War Diary	Folkestone	04/05/1915	04/05/1915
War Diary	Boulogne	04/05/1915	04/05/1915
War Diary	Berguette	05/05/1915	05/05/1915
War Diary	Lilette	05/05/1915	06/05/1915
War Diary	Calonne Sur La Lys	07/05/1915	14/05/1915
War Diary	Meteren	14/05/1915	14/05/1915
War Diary	Meteren	18/05/1915	18/05/1915
War Diary	La Gorgue	19/05/1915	19/05/1915
War Diary	Locon	20/05/1915	20/05/1915
War Diary	Trenches	25/05/1915	31/05/1915
Heading	War Diary 1/4th Battalion Loyal North Lancs June 1915 Also Report on Operations 15th-16th June '15		
War Diary		01/06/1915	25/06/1915
War Diary	Trenches	25/06/1915	30/06/1915
Miscellaneous	References To Attached Trench Map	05/06/1915	05/06/1915
Miscellaneous	Account Of The Attack On The German Salient W Of The Rue D'ouvert On The Night Of June 15-16	15/06/1915	15/06/1915
Map	Sketch Map Of Trenches		
Miscellaneous			
Heading	51st Division July-August 1/4 L.N. Lancs Vol I		
War Diary		03/07/1915	31/08/1915
Heading	51st Division War Diary Of 1/4th Loyal North Lancashire Regt. From Sept 4th To Sept 30th Vol II		
War Diary		04/09/1915	18/09/1915
War Diary	Aveluy	19/09/1915	21/09/1915
War Diary	Martinsart	22/09/1915	30/09/1915
Heading	51st Division War Diary Of 1/4th Battalion The Loyal North Lancashire Regiment From 1st October 1915 To 31st October 1915 Vol III		
War Diary	Aveluy	01/10/1915	05/10/1915
War Diary	Trenches	05/10/1915	21/10/1915
War Diary	Aveluy	22/10/1914	31/10/1914
Heading	51st Division 1/4th Loyal Nth Lancs Rgt. Nov Vol IV		
Heading	War Diary Of 1/7th Loyal North Lancashire Regiment From 1st November 1915 To 30th November 1915		
War Diary	Lesdos	01/11/1915	07/11/1915
War Diary	Bouzincourt	08/11/1915	18/11/1915
War Diary	Authville	18/11/1915	24/11/1915
War Diary	Trenches	24/11/1915	28/11/1915
War Diary	Bouzincourt	29/11/1915	30/11/1915

Heading	War Diary Of The 1/4th Loyal North Lancashire Regiment From 1st December 1915 To 31st December 1915 Vol V		
War Diary	Bouzincourt	01/12/1915	05/12/1915
War Diary	Trenches	06/12/1915	16/12/1915
War Diary	Bouzincourt	17/12/1915	22/12/1915
War Diary	Trenches	22/12/1915	27/12/1915
War Diary	Authville	28/12/1915	29/12/1915
War Diary	Trenches	29/12/1915	29/12/1915
War Diary	Authville Trenches	30/12/1915	31/12/1915

WO95/2887/4

1/4 Battalion Loyal North
Lancashire Regiment

51ST DIVISION
154TH INFY BDE

1-4TH BN LOY. NTH LANCS
19 MAY - DEC 1915

To 55 DIV 164 BDE

Army Form C. 2118.

1/4th Loyal North Lancashire Regt
164th Infantry Brigade.

WAR DIARY
or
INTELLIGENCE SUMMARY
(Erase heading not required.)

Instructions regarding War Diaries and Intelligence Summaries are contained in F. S. Regs., Part II. and the Staff Manual respectively. Title pages will be prepared in manuscript.

Hour, Date, Place			Summary of Events and Information	Remarks and references to Appendices
			Original	
1.5 a.m.	2.6.15.	BEDFORD.	3 Officers, 104 Rank & File & the whole of the Regimental Transport entrained at BALLAST PIT SIDING.	
6.40 a.m	do	SOUTHAMPTON	Arrived at SOUTHAMPTON DOCKS, embarked S.S. "ROSSETTI", sailed at 4.30 p.m.	
3.0 a.m	do	HAVRE	Arrived at HAVRE, disembarked & moved to No. 5 Rest Camp at 9.30 a.m.	
1.0 a.m	3.5.15	HAVRE	Details & Regimental Transport entrained at POINT 41, GARE DE MARCHANDISE.	
7+2 p.m } 8.15 p.m }	3.6.15	BEDFORD	The Battalion (less details & Regimental Transport) entrained in two trains at BALLAST PIT SIDING.	
12.8 40 a.m 1. 15 a.m }	4.5.15. do	do	The Battalion arrived at FOLKESTONE, & embarked in S.S. "ONWARD" immediately.	
1.30 a.m	do	FOLKESTONE	S.S. "ONWARD" sailed from FOLKESTONE.	
3.0 a.m	do	BOULOGNE	Arrived at BOULOGNE, was disembarked, and marched to OSTROHOVE Rest Camp.	
6.30 p.m	do	do	The Battalion paraded and marched to PONT DE BRIQUES Railway Station.	
8.10 p.m	do	do	The Battalion entrained, & joined details & Regimental Transport which had arrived in the same train from HAVRE.	

Army Form C. 2118.

WAR DIARY
or
INTELLIGENCE SUMMARY
(Erase heading not required.)

1/4th Loyal North Lancashire Reg.
154th Infantry Brigade.

Instructions regarding War Diaries and Intelligence Summaries are contained in F.S. Regs., Part II. and the Staff Manual respectively. Title pages will be prepared in manuscript.

Hour, Date, Place			Summary of Events and Information	Remarks and references to Appendices
2.30 a.m.	5.5.15.	BERGUETTE	The Battalion detrained at BERGUETTE.	
4.0 a.m.	do	do	The Battalion commenced its march to LILLETTE.	
6.0 a.m.	do	LILLETTE	The Battalion arrived & went into billets.	
7.15 p.m.	6/5.15	do	Orders were received to move at 8 p.m.	Appendix I. (Bde Opn Order No. 2)
9.47 p.m.	do	LILLERS	The Battalion reached the starting point at LILLERS.	
4.0 a.m.	7.5.15.	CALONNE (SUR LA LYS)	The Battalion arrived and went into billets along the ROBECQ Road at CALONNE.	
9.30 p.m.	do	do	The Brigadier summoned a conference of Commanding Officers and Adjutants at Brigade Headquarters. A state of readiness to move at an hour's notice was ordered.	App. II. (Bde Opn Order No. 4)
12.30 a.m.	14.5.15	do	Orders were received to be ready to march at 8.30 a.m.	
9.11 a.m.	do	do	The Battalion moved to its starting point in CALONNE.	
2.0 p.m.	do	HETEREN	The Battalion arrived at the outskirts of the town. As soon as billets had been arranged, the battalion went into billets on the East North east side of the town.	

WAR DIARY or INTELLIGENCE SUMMARY

Army Form C. 2118.

1/4 Royal North Lancs Reg.t
154 Inf: Bde.

Hour, Date, Place		Summary of Events and Information	Remarks and references to Appendices
5.10 p.m	MAY 18th METEREN	The Battalion marched with the Brigade to new billets at LA GORGUE. The route lay through VIEUX BERQUIN & NEUF BERQUIN. Owing to a delay of two hours on the road the Brigade did not arrive till 3.a.m. The men rested all day. 18 men were detached to the Tunnelling Company R.E. The 2/5th Lancash. Fusiliers, one of the Battalions of the Brigade, left to join St OMER.	
9.a.m	19th LA GORGUE	Marched to billets on the E side of the canal at LOCON. The Battalion remained here until 25th inst. The men carried out physical training, bayonet fighting and short route marches. Grenade throwing Machine Guns & Signalling training commenced.	
7.p.m	20th LOCON	The battalion moved out of billets and relieved Black Watch in the trenches. The Sector allotted to the Battalion lay about one mile W.N.W. of FESTUBERT the Bn being right rested on LA QUINQUE RUE the left on the road from RUE DE L'EPINETTE to FERME COUR D'AVOINE A & D Coys and M.G. Section occupied the Fire Trenches C Coy the Support Trench	
	25th TRENCHES.		

Army Form C. 2118.

1/4 Royal North Lancs Regt
154 Inf. Bde.

WAR DIARY
or
INTELLIGENCE SUMMARY

(Erase heading not required.)

Instructions regarding War Diaries and Intelligence Summaries are contained in F.S. Regs., Part II. and the Staff Manual respectively. Title pages will be prepared in manuscript.

Hour, Date, Place	Summary of Events and Information	Remarks and references to Appendices
May	and B Coy the Reserve Trench. The fire trench had only recently been constructed and on the right was about 150 yards short of LA QUINQUE RUE. The SUPPORT TRENCH was an old German trench. No wire had been put up. German trenches opposite to us ran from near N.14 to P.14, thence through the buildings P.15, P.16, to Q.12 and Q.11. Q.10 and Q.9 was not occupied	
2.10 am 26 TRENCHES	Relief was limpingly carried out. It had been considerably delayed by a report that the trenches were being shelled and it was nearly midnight before the leading company entered. An intermittent fire. The night passed off quietly. High explosive shells was of by the shrapnel and High explosive shells kept up by the enemy all day. The fire at no time was severe. 2 men were wounded.	
27.	The trenches were shelled off + on all day considerable field fire without damage. by shrapnel of fire trench was much improved	

Army Form C. 2118.

1/4 Royal North Lancs Regt.
154 Inf Bde.

WAR DIARY
or
INTELLIGENCE SUMMARY
(Erase heading not required.)

Hour, Date, Place	Summary of Events and Information	Remarks and references to Appendices
May 28 3 p.m.	The fire trench was heavily shelled in the morning by shrapnel. Heavy shelling. 6 men were wounded.	
9-45 pm	A working party commenced to prolong on trench to the right to join up with the Canadian left. The R.E. bridged a ditch in front of our fire trench.	
29	The enemy kept up fairly heavy shrapnel fire & 2 men were wounded. A working party of 200 men with a covering party of 25 men started a new trench running from bridge (constructed last night) to the Canadians in a S S E direction.	
30	Careful hearings were taken on flashes of enemy guns during night disclosing them to be at or near a pit known as N 20 at a range of about 1400 yds from our fire trench. A heavy gun fire & was kept up by enemy throughout day. Working parties continued work commenced previous night.	See ILLIES, VIOLAINES, FESTUBERT trench map.

Army Form C. 2118.

1/4 Royal North Lancs Regt.
154 Inf. Bde.

WAR DIARY
or
INTELLIGENCE SUMMARY
(Erase heading not required.)

Instructions regarding War Diaries and Intelligence Summaries are contained in F.S. Regs., Part II. and the Staff Manual respectively. Title pages will be prepared in manuscript.

Hour, Date, Place	Summary of Events and Information	Remarks and references to Appendices
11 p.m. May 30	Message received that Divisional guns would heavily bombard enemy trenches at 12.15 a.m. & 2.15 a.m. for one hour. News of this was communicated to all working parties. Above bombardment was punctually carried out. Enemy replied by shelling our trenches without serious damage.	
31	Men 1 killed 5 wounded. 2/Lt H.X. BRYCE-SMITH was wounded. Enemy's fire died down.	
3.20 a.m.	Fresh outbreak of enemy fire which damaged our fire trenches in several places. This was soon made good.	
11 a.m.	[struck through] Position was reconnoitred by 58th VAUGHAN'S RIFLES with one Coy 1/8th BLACK WATCH in reserve. Billets were taken up in village of CORNET MALKO ½ mile N of TOCON Church. The battalion rested all day. [struck through]	

154/51

WAR DIARY

1/4th Battalion,
Loyal North Lancs:
June 1915.

Also Report on Operations.
15th – 16th June '15.

Army Form C. 2118.

1/4 L.N. Lancs Regt.
154 Inf. Bde.

154/51

WAR DIARY
or
INTELLIGENCE SUMMARY
(Erase heading not required.)

Instructions regarding War Diaries and Intelligence Summaries are contained in F.S. Regs., Part II. and the Staff Manual respectively. Title pages will be prepared in manuscript.

Hour	Date	Place	Summary of Events and Information	Remarks and references to Appendices
	1915 June 1		Very quiet day.	
11 p.m.			2 men wounded. Battalion was relieved by 58th VAUGHAN'S RIFLES with one Coy 1/8th BLACK WATCH in reserve.	
4-30 a.m.	2		Men went into billets at CORNET MALO 1/2 mile N.W. LOCON church. Battalion rested all day.	
6 p.m.	4		The Battalion moved to fresh billets via LA BASSÉE canal between CALONNE + ROBECQ.	
	5		A Brigade Grenadier Company was formed. LIEUT E.M. GREGSON + 20 other ranks were posted to the Grenadier Company. LIEUT W SMITH with 4 men to Trench Mortar class.	
7 p.m.	6		Battalion moved back to old billets at CORNET MALO.	
	7		Companies carried out manual training. Weather unusually hot.	

WAR DIARY
or
INTELLIGENCE SUMMARY

(Erase heading not required.)

Army Form C. 2118.

1/4 L.N. Lancs Regt.
154 Inf. Bde.

Hour, Date, Place	Summary of Events and Information	Remarks and references to Appendices
June 8	Very heavy thunderstorm accompanied by hail & heavy rain. Roads very muddy.	
9, 7.30 p.m	The Battalion left CORNET MALO to relieve 1/7th "BLACK WATCH" in the trenches running along RUE DE BOIS, RUE DE L'EPINETTE through FESTUBERT village & down QUINQUE RUE for about 800 yds. Our front extended about 700 yds. Our right resting on QUINQUE RUE. The 1/8th LIVERPOOL IRISH occupied the fire & support trenches.	
10	Two or three heavy thunderstorms soon turned the trenches into a quagmire, which rendered progress for night working parties very difficult. 7 men wounded.	
11, 10·45 p.m	The Battalion was relieved by 1/7th BLACK WATCH and went into billets at LE CORNET MALO Q 33 which were reached at 5 a.m. June 12. Relieved 163 Bde.	BETHUNE 36 A (combined Series) 36 B.T.C. second edition
12	in the trenches on QUINQUE RUE.	
13	The Battalion returned to the trenches resting on the left of the B & C Coys in fire trench A Coy in support " D " " " "	

Army Form C. 2118.

1/4th L.N. Lanc. Reg.t
154 Inf. Bde.

WAR DIARY
or
INTELLIGENCE SUMMARY
(Erase heading not required.)

Instructions regarding War Diaries and Intelligence Summaries are contained in F. S. Regs., Part II. and the Staff Manual respectively. Title pages will be prepared in manuscript.

Hour, Date, Place	Summary of Events and Information	Remarks and references to Appendices
11.45pm June 13	During relief 2/Lt. A.T. HOUGHTON & one man were wounded. The 1/6 Scottish Rifles were on our left & the 2²ⁿᵈ Brigade on our right.	
14.	We were warned for an attack and Operation orders were issued by the Brigade. During the day & the following day the men were busy bringing up sandbags, bridges & stout to be used during the attack. Our artillery commenced the 48hrs bombardment about dawn which was directed chiefly on the enemy's barbed wire entanglements. A heavy fire was kept up throughout the day the German reply with bursts of shrapnel & his high explosive shells, mainly directed against our communication trenches. During the day we lost ___. The bombardment continued throughout the night with the exception of two short stoppages along the front & on both flanks.	See Operation Order No. 10 issued by Brig: General G.L. HIBBERT commanding 154 Inf. Bde.
15.	See attached account of the battle.	

Army Form C. 2118.

1/4 Loyal North Lancs Regt.
154 Inf Bde.

WAR DIARY
or
INTELLIGENCE SUMMARY
(Erase heading not required.)

Instructions regarding War Diaries and Intelligence Summaries are contained in F.S. Regs., Part II. and the Staff Manual respectively. Title pages will be prepared in manuscript.

Hour, Date, Place	Summary of Events and Information	Remarks and references to Appendices
June 16. 7a.m.	The remnants of the Battalion were relieved by 1/8th at LE TOURET on the RUE DE BOIS.	
10 a.m.	The Battalion marched to billets at LE CORNET MALO. Arrived in billets.	
2 p.m.		
17 to 21	The battalion was occupied in reorganising & re-equipping.	26A35, 26B35 26B.N.E. 36.N.W. Contoured sheets Second Edition.
22	The Battalion moved into Brigade Reserve in billets near LACOUTURE. Working party of 200 men sent to trenches.	× 3d + 4e Batteries
5 p.m. 24.	The 51st Division rejoined the Indian CORPS.	
25.	The Battalion marched with the Brigade to ESTAIRES via:- LESTREM and LA GORGUE. Roads exceedingly good. Arrived at ESTAIRE at 10 a.m. Went into billets.	App III (See Bde Opn Orders) No. 11 24/6/15.

1247 W 8299 200,000 (E) 8/14 J.B.C. & A. Forms/C. 2118/11.

Army Form C. 2118.

1/4 Loyal North Lancs Regt.
154 Inf. Bde.

WAR DIARY
or
INTELLIGENCE SUMMARY

(Erase heading not required.)

Hour, Date, Place	Summary of Events and Information	Remarks and references to Appendices
7p.m June 25 TRENCHES	Battalion left ESTAIRE and marched via LAVENTIE to take over trenches from 1/5th MIDDLESEX Regt at FAUQUISSART. Our front extended from a pt 200 yds N.W. of RUE D'ENFER for about 400 yds. 1/5 TT FLANK 1/6 SCOTTISH RIFLES were on our LEFT flank 1/4 R LANCASTER REGT on our right.	See AUBERS Trench map FAUQUISSART map
26 to 30	Very quiet time. Few shells were fired at our position & the line although snipers were very active at times. During this period 1 man was killed & 3 wounded. The weather was exceedingly hot. Much useful work was done in building up parados, strengthening parapet & shelter trenches, making new communication trenches to support trench which was being built 60 yds in rear of fire trench.	

SECRET.
No 9109
HIGHLAND
DIVISION.

SECRET.

References to attached trench map.

REPORT ON THE PROJECTED ATTACK OF RUE D'OUVERT.

1.   The attack to be carried out from our present front line trenches, and to consist of two distinct lines of advance,

(a) from L 8 and our trench running north, to attack L 9, L 10, L 13,

(b) from our trench at M 6 towards M 8, to attack L 12 and the houses in that locality.

2.   The right attack, (a), will be undertaken by the 154th Brigade, and the left attack, (b), by the 152nd Brigade. The respective Brigadiers will command these attacks.

3.   Each of these attacks will be made by about $1\frac{1}{2}$ companies infantry in the front line, who would be assembled in the front trenches for this purpose. The supports in each instance will consist of the remainder of the Battalion disposed in support trenches in rear. The garrison of the front line would thus form the actual attacking force. The 152nd Brigade is now in the trenches, and the 154th Brigade will go in to-morrow night. Arrnagements will be made so that the troops who make the assault will have been not more than one day in the trenches when the time comes.

4.   A second battalion in each brigade will be in reserve in the old German and British lines. A third battalion from each brigade will be standing by in some convenient place, west of RUE DE L'EPINETTE. The fourth battalion of each brigade will be in the fire and support trenches out of which no attack is to be made, and will continue to form the garrison after the attack has started. These latter battalions will be required to assist by their fire, and to

hold the line in case of a failure followed by a counter-attack.

5. The artillery arrangements are being worked out separately. To support the attack effectively, the following tasks are required from the guns:-

(a) A bombardment, with high explosive shell, of the German fire trenches opposite the points of attack.

(b) A bombardment, with high explosive, of likely supporting points and machine gun positions immediately behind their front line.

(c) Wire cutting, with shrapnel, along the front to be attacked.

(d) A bombardment, with high explosive or shrapnel, of the German trenches which are not to be attacked while the attack is taking place. This should include particularly those lengths of trenches from which an enfilade fire could be brought to bear, which are from M 10 for 350 yards to the S.W., the trench between L 9 and L 12, and the trench opposite K 7, K 8. It should also include M 10 and the farm on the RUE DE MARAIS 300 yards S.W. of that place.

(e) Barrages on the line of approach.

(f) Counter-battery guns.

6. The C.R.E. of the Division will arrange the necessary preparations for the infantry attack in the way of communication exits from the fire trenches and bridges for the ditches. A section of R.E. will follow the right attack at a short interval, and will be employed in cutting a fresh length of trench to join up our post at L 8 with the German trench which runs towards L 10. A section of R.E., assisted by a working party, will similarly be employed in continuing and improving an old trench which runs from

near

near L 12 towards M 6. Each of these R.E. sections will be placed in some convenient support trench, ready to move up at once if the infantry attacks are successful. Carrying parties for the R.E. will be provided from infantry in reserve.

7. The Brigade commanders concerned are considering the plans in detail. Their proposals have not yet been submitted, but the following points are to be arranged:-

(a) All infantry officers and N.C.O's who are to take part in the attack must be given some information of the ground. It is proposed to issue small sketches from Divisional Headquarters.
(b) Signals to show the points reached by the infantry advance.
(c) Routes for the supporting troops, R.E. and carrying parties to be marked.
(d) Duplicate wires, advanced report centres, and routes for orderlies are to be prepared and arranged for.
(e) Supplies of ammunition, bombs and rations?
(f) Blocking parties, which will include bombers.
(g) The position of battalion bombers during the attack.
(h) Issue of extra wire cutters.
(i) Arrangements for synchronising watches with R.A.

Major General,
Commanding
51st (Highland) Division.

5th June, 1915.

Account of the attack on the German Salient W of the RUE D'OUVERT on the night of June 15-16.

June 15th "Original"

At 11 a.m in reply to an enquiry from the artillery as to amount of damage done to the enemy's wire by the artillery fire on our line of advance. Major NICKSON replied that most of the wire had been destroyed. Capt & Adjt C.C NORMAN reported to the same effect but added that the wire in front of the enemy's main trench could not be observed clearly from our fire trench.

The bombardment continued as on the previous day, with the Germans still only occasionally replying. The German wire, fire trenches, sap head & the houses to our left front were kept under a continuous fire while an advanced mountain battery played on the enemy's parapet.

B Coy was withdrawn from the fire to the

support trench to the right of D Coy whilst C Coy moved to the right of the fire trench making room for the charging company of the 1/6 CAMERONIANS on their left.

Orders were received in the afternoon that the British bombardment would greatly increase in intensity at 5-30pm & would continue so until 6 p.m. For this first 1/2 hour the fire would be concentrated on the enemy's barbed wire. At 6 p.m. the guns would lift on to the enemy's fire trench and shell this solely for 3 minutes. At 6-3 pm the enemy's communication trenches would be shelled for 1 minute & their main trench from 6-4 to 6-15. At 6-15 the guns would lift into the road & would shell this intensley for 1/2 hour. At 6-45 pm the artillery would form a barrage beyond the road.

Punctually at 5-30 p.m. the bombardment became terrific and the enemy's positions were subjected to a perfect rain of shells. B and D companies moved up the communication trenches towards the fire trench & A moved up to the supporting trench from the reserve line.

During this time the German artillery which up to now had been merely desultory became very intense. The communication trenches were subjected to a murderous fire & it was with great difficulty that the supporting troops made their way up to the fire trench.

At 6p.m precisely C Coy charged from the fire trench.
The leading platoon was a composite one made up from Nos 9 & 12 for strength, under command of 2/Lt P. PARKER. N° 10 platoon under 2/Lt CRAVEN followed at 100 yds interval & N° 11 under command of 2/Lt W. A. DAVIS followed N° 10.
Under a withering fire they climbed the parapet formed to the left & charged. This was done in perfect line & within 3 minutes they were in possession of the German trench

Their losses were chiefly from rifle and machine gun fire, which must have come from the enemy's main trench & not from the advanced trench of the salient since they found most of the Germans sheltering in "dug outs" in the advanced trench, & these were dealt with by the bombers.

The bombing parties were divided into two groups
(a) (Right group) 1/4 Royal Lanc. Reg.t under Lieut TAYLOR
(b) (Left group) 1/6th Scottish Rifles under Lieut HAY

These bombing parties supported by the various parties told off to them did magnificent work & penetrated right through the road to a much greater distance than ever the assaulting battalions reached.

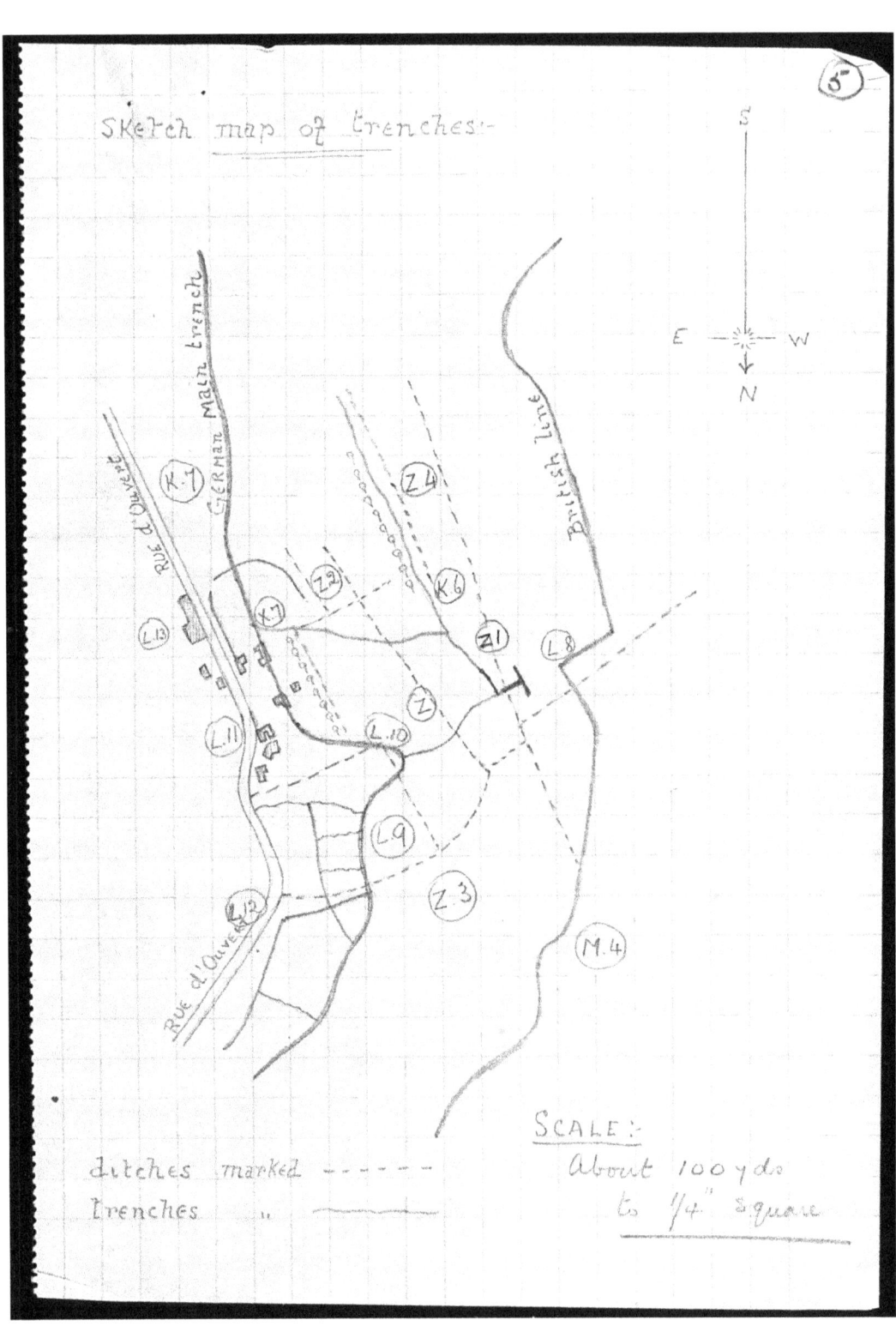

Roughly it may be said that the centre of the attack was — (L8) see map —. The two leading platoons of C Coy with their left directing the whole attack, charged the German T head sap direct to their front, & taking this in the rush swept on to the German fire trench.

The 1/6th SCOTTISH RIFLES charged at the same time with their right resting on the German communication trench.

The German trench was taken with ease. The bombing parties extended outwards down past (Z1) (K6) & (Z4). Their orders were to push ahead as far as possible as the 7th Division, as detailed, would be attacking at the same time.

Another bombing party were to break off towards the German main trench at (X7). The other main party of bombers went towards (L10) up the communication trench.

The bombers carried red flags to show the artillery the furthermost

points reached by the infantry. A red rocket was also to be fired when the infantry reached the houses in the road at (L11).
Unfortunately the artillery observing officers could see nothing on account of the smoke & dust which completely hid the scenes of operations from view.

Telephonic communication soon broke down & messages had to be sent by relays of orderlies.
Lieut ORD was in charge of this at (L8).

The course of the battle becomes a little obscure. The next company was B & there seems no connected account of what actually happened as all the officers became casulties. B Coy men state that they had to cross a deep ditch with wire entanglements at the bottom. This must have been the ditch in front of the German fire trench at (Z.1).
At this point the German artillery

redoubled in intensity on the deploying companies & whereas C Coy had suffered chiefly from rifle & machine gun fire. B. D & A Coys suffered more from shell fire.

B Coy seem to have reinforced C Coy on our right.

D Company coming up the now badly damaged fire & communication trenches were sent to reinforce the front line on the left

Both B & D Coys moved to support in lines of platoons through a gap in the fire trench

Meantime the attack had swept on past the enemy's fire trench along the communication trenches & must have carried the main trench but for coming up against a mass of uncut barbed wire. During the latter period we lost a big number of men from enfilade fire from somewhere about X7 & Z2.

The above mentioned barbed wire lay on the EAST side of the ditch which runs parallel to the German main trench SE from (L10). Capt. NORMAN had said that this part could not be observed from our fire trench.

Heavy Machine gun fire came from a house about (L11).

The position then about 7 p.m was as follows.

Barbed wire: ―――
trenches: ―――
ditches: - - - - - -

The 1/6th SCOTTISH RIFLES were attacking on our left with their right resting on the Sap head at (L.8). Their advance was checked very early on by uncut barbed wire which ran along the northern edge of the German communication trench. They lay in the open under very galling fire & lost heavily in attempting to cut it. Unable to proceed they attempted to get up the communication trench running towards (L10). At 7pm they were in this trench when the 1/4 L.N. Lanc Regt. were checked.

This trench was also used by the Germans as a fire trench as it faced obliquely the British trench at (M.4). This change of front formed an angle at L10. The 1/6 Scottish Rifles facing NORTH while the 1/4th L.N. Lanc Regt. faced N.E.

The Ditch.
The 1/4 L.N. Lanc Regt. not being able to advance were ordered to "dig in" in the ditch.
This ditch was bordered on the EAST

side by a row of pollard willows.
On the left the ditch was comparatively
dry with a slight protecting bank
on the E side, but the further away
to the right the more a quagmire
it became. In some places it
was thigh deep in water.
(the ditch)
It afforded comparative safety
after the advance, because it was
too near the German trench
for their artillery to fire

The men had to rely chiefly on
the entrenching tool for digging
in as most of the shovels
& sandbags which came up with
the supports were lost on the
way up to the front line.

The battalion entrenched itself
in this ditch as well as was
possible, & it was rapidly going
dark. A Coy as it came up was
sent to the right of the line
to strengthen & extend it & to get
in touch with the 7th Division
on our right. Several parties were

sent out to find the 7th Division position but without success. At dusk one company of the 1/4th ROYAL LANCASTER Regt under the command of Capt Barrow came up to reinforce.

Major NICKSON 1/4th L.N.L Regt was in command of this front line. The Colonel (Lt Colonel R. HINDLE) was wounded early on, & Major F.W. FOLEY took over command & established his H.Q. at (L8).

About 11 p.m the German artillery slackened, which had been shelling the communication & support trenches all the time.

A machine gun had been placed in position ~~—— ——~~ near (L10), the remainder having been put out of action during the advance.

The extreme right flank near X.7 was bent back to protect that flank.

The line was a bad one.
Both flanks were in the air.
We were not in touch with the 7th Division
& enfilade fire was coming from the
right flank.
The ditch was waterlogged & clearly
marked by the row of willows.
Spades, picks, sandbags & bombs
were lacking & all the bombers
had become casualties.
The reserve of bombs near L8 could
not be found.
A party of 33 bombers were sent
from the reserve trench, but all
were became casualties with the
exception of 5.

Major NICKSON sent back explaining
the position to Major Foley at (L8)
& asked for instructions, before these
could arrive the Germans counter-
attacked.

About midnight the Germans
threw up flares in large numbers
& shortly afterwards they commenced
the counter attack.

They began by bombing at (1.10) immediately putting the our machine gun out of action, & breaking connection with the 1/6th Scottish Rifles. At the same time they bombed down the communication trench (X7) & commenced throwing bombs across the open from their main trench.

We could get nothing from the rear, & to remain isolated as we were would have meant the wiping out of the whole line.

Orders were given to withdraw from the position.

At a point about (Z) on the map, a mixed body of men lined the shell craters & held up the enemy for 2 hours, losing heavily in doing so. These men eventually retired in the morning mist towards the sap S.W of (L8)

June 16th
The attacking battalions were withdrawn to the reserve trenches

about 5 a.m. & the lines were taken over by the 1/8th LIVERPOOL IRISH.

The battalion assembled at LE TOURET. & had breakfast & a rum ration issued.

243 men answered the roll.

Casualties:- Officers:-

Lt. Colonel	R. HINDLE.	Wounded.
Capt. Adjt.	C.C. NORMAN.	"
Capt.	C.G.R. HIBBERT	missing
"	J.H. PEAK.	"
"	J.L. WHITFIELD	died of wounds 27/6/15
Lieut.	W. SMITH	" " " 17/6/15
"	K.H. MOORE	Wounded.
"	J.L. BRINDLE.	"
2/Lt	E. RAWSTHORNE	Killed
"	W.A. DAVIS.	"
"	P. PARKER.	Wounded.
"	N. CRAVEN.	"

Other ranks: Killed.   Wounded   missing
                 19.   255   145.

121/6539

134 51st Division

John & August
114 N. Lancs.
Vol I
From 2nd May to 31st August 1915

Mr

Army Form C. 2118.

1/4 Royal North Lancs Regt.
154th Inf. Bde.

WAR DIARY
or
INTELLIGENCE SUMMARY

(Erase heading not required.)

Hour, Date, Place	Summary of Events and Information	Remarks and references to Appendices
10 p.m. July 8	The Battalion was relieved by 1/7th GORDON HIGHLANDERS, marched to billets at LA-GORGUE. Billets were situated on ESTAIRES-LA BASSEE Road. Working parties were required every night & the Battalion carried out Company training for a few hours daily.	
9 TRENCHES	The Battalion returned to trenches S.W of RUE D'ENFER, on right flank resting on RUE D'ENFER and extending about 400yds to the left. * Very quiet time, we silenced the enemy's snipers very quickly. One enemy trench mortared the regiment on our life at times without serious damage.	* 1 Killed 3 wounded
10 to 16		
10 p.m. 16	Relieved by 1/4 R Lancaster Regt & went into Brigade reserve along RUE BACQUEROT about 1000 yds behind the trenches. Also took over MASSELOT'S CELLAR posts which were in 2nd line / defence.	

WAR DIARY or INTELLIGENCE SUMMARY

Army Form C. 2118.

(Erase heading not required.)

Hour, Date, Place	Summary of Events and Information	Remarks and references to Appendices
July 17 to 22.	The Battalion carried out close order drill, companies were practised in bomb throwing etc.	
23	2nd MIDDLESEX relieved us and we marched via ESTAIRE to NEUF BERQUIN to billets arriving at 2.45 a.m. 26th.	
25.	2/Lt LINDSAY with one other rank left ESTAIRE with Brigade billeting party for new area.	
27 2.p.m. 3-3 p.m. 4-3 p.m. 8-10 p.m.	The Battalion left for LA GORGUE station. Battalion entrained. Train started. Arrived CALAIS. One hour's halt. The men made tea at boilers which were placed along the line & obtained refreshment at a Y.M.C.A. stall which was greatly appreciated.	
28 9-3 p.m. 1-30 a.m.	Left for AMIENS. Arrived ABBEVILLE. One hour's halt.	

Army Form C. 2118.

WAR DIARY
or
INTELLIGENCE SUMMARY

(Erase heading not required.)

1/4 Loyal North Lancs.
154 Inf. Bde.

Instructions regarding War Diaries and Intelligence Summaries are contained in F. S. Regs, Part II. and the Staff Manual respectively. Title pages will be prepared in manuscript.

Hour, Date, Place	Summary of Events and Information	Remarks and references to Appendices
July 28 5 a.m.	Passed through AMIENS.	
6-5 a.m.	Arrived CORBIE & detrained. Marched to billets at RIBEMONT. 1/4 R LANCASTER Regt, 1/6 SCOTTISH RIFLES, were also billeted here. 1/8 LIVERPOOL IRISH & 2/5th LANCASHIRE FUSILIERS were billeted at CORBIE.	
31	The Division took over trenches from the French. R LANCASTER Regt in Brigade Reserve at AVELUY. The battalion was in Divisional Reserve.	
8 p.m.	Marched from RIBEMONT to billets at MARTINSART.	
11-40 p.m.	Arrived at MARTINSART. The men were billeted in barns, but the majority preferred to bivouac in orchards.	

Army Form C. 2118.

1/4th L.N.Lanc Regt
/154 Inf Bde

WAR DIARY
or
INTELLIGENCE SUMMARY
(Erase heading not required.)

Hour, Date, Place	Summary of Events and Information	Remarks and references to Appendices
August		
2	2/Lt. G. NORWOOD joined the battalion.	
3	The battalion remained in Divisional reserve	
5	at MARTINSART. continued Company training	
7	bomb throwing etc. During this time the	
	battalion took over the guarding of the	
	village. The H.Q of the 152nd brigade were	
	stationed here also the 1/1st Highland	
6	R.E Field Company.	
	Coy officers were sent up to look round	
	the trenches which at we were taking over.	
	2/Lt. W.R HAGGAS reported from 2/4th L.N.Lanc	
	Regt bringing 5 N.C.Os These who had	
4	been wounded from the same	
	The battalion left for the trenches and	
	relieved the 4th LANCASHIRE FUSILEERS in	
7.pm 7	Section B. A.B.C Companies were in the	
	fire trench D Coy being in support at	
	POSTE DE LESDOS	

Army Form C. 2118.

1/4 L.N. Lanc Regt.
154 Ind[?] Bde

WAR DIARY
or
INTELLIGENCE SUMMARY
(Erase heading not required.)

Instructions regarding War Diaries and Intelligence Summaries are contained in F. S. Regs., Part II. and the Staff Manual respectively. Title pages will be prepared in manuscript.

Hour, Date, Place	Summary of Events and Information	Remarks and references to Appendices
August 7.	The 1/6th SCOTTISH RIFLES occupied the right half of sector B the whole sector being under the command of Lt Colonel F.W. FOLEY 1/4 L.N. Lanc Ry. The HQ of the battalion were in the wood (S of AUTHUILLE) The trenches were cut in the solid chalk very few sandbags being used. The French had made the dug outs very comfortable & they were nearly all splinter proof. The trenches in this sector were well protected by barbed wire.	
10 p.m. 9.	A thunderstorm with torrential rain churned the trenches into mud for the next few days and made things very unpleasant	
11.	First half of 7 went to England on leave. 2 other ranks wounded This sector was very quiet the whole time nothing worthy of note happened.	

Army Form C. 2118.

1/4 L.N. Lanc Regt
154 Inf Bde.

WAR DIARY
or
INTELLIGENCE SUMMARY
(Erase heading not required.)

Instructions regarding War Diaries and Intelligence Summaries are contained in F.S. Regs., Part II. and the Staff Manual respectively. Title pages will be prepared in manuscript.

Hour, Date, Place	Summary of Events and Information	Remarks and references to Appendices
August 14	The battalion was relieved by 2/5th LANCASHIRE FUSILEERS in Sector A which is S.E. of LA BOISELLE relieving 1/8th LIVERPOOL IRISH. C & D Coys occupied the fire trench. A & B coys being in support at POSTE DONNEZ. All four Companies of the 1/4th KINGS OWN Regt were in the remainder of the sector on our left, the whole sector being under command of Lt.Col F. WILSON FOLEY. On our right was the 153rd BRIGADE.	
17th	B Coy took over from C Coy the latter coming to the supports. 18th draft arrived from England. Lt. Colonel R. HINDLE returned & took over the command of the battalion.	
21st	The battalion was relieved by 1/8th LIVERPOOL IRISH who took over the whole of the fire trench in sector A. Two companies of the KINGS OWN were in support at POSTE DONNEZ. Two coys in support at POSTE LESBOS. 1/4th L.N. Lanc Regt went into billets at AVELUY. During the whole of this period the weather was fine and we suffered only one casualty.	

Army Form C. 2118.

WAR DIARY
or
INTELLIGENCE SUMMARY
(Erase heading not required.)

1/4 L.N. Lanc Regt
154 Inf. Bde.

Hour, Date, Place	Summary of Events and Information	Remarks and references to Appendices
August 14 to 21	During this period the entire rations were cooked on the cookers which were stationed under the lee of the hill East of AVELUY. This was a long way to carry rations to the fire trench & another scheme is under consideration. During this period men in the fire trench had hot tea or soup served out at 12-30 midnight which was greatly appreciated. Also 1/3 of the men were allowed to sleep at night.	
22 to 28	Remained in Brigade reserve in AVELUY. During this period we found all road guards. One company found the guards, one Coy outlying party, one Coy carried out training.	
22	Were on a working party, the fourth picquet, & received a draft from 2/4th L.N. Lanc Regt of 101 other ranks.	
23	Received 4 officers. 2/Lt A.B. BRATTON from 3rd L.N. Lanc Regt " H.W. STRONG " H.W.J.S. WALKER from 11th L.N. Lanc Regt 2 Lt M.W. NOLAN	

Army Form C. 2118.

WAR DIARY
or
INTELLIGENCE SUMMARY

(Erase heading not required.)

1/4 = L.N. Lanc Regt.
154 Inf: Bde.

Hour, Date, Place	Summary of Events and Information	Remarks and references to Appendices
August 28th	Relieved 2/5th Lanc FUSILIERS in Sector B. A. C & D companies in the firing line with the 1/6th SCOTTISH RIFLES on our left. The whole sector under command of Lt Colonel R HINDLE at POSTE LESDOS. B Coy 1/4 = L.N. Lanc was in support at POSTE LESDOS.	
28 to 31	Nothing to report. Rained heavily every night which made the trenches very wet muddy. Fine during the day. Casualties for this period 4 O.R. wounded	

51st Division

121/699

CONFIDENTIAL.

WAR DIARY

OF

1/4th LOYAL NORTH LANCASHIRE REGT.

FROM SEPT 4th TO SEPT 30th.

Vol II

WAR DIARY
or
INTELLIGENCE SUMMARY

(Erase heading not required.)

Army Form C. 2118.

1/4 K.N. Lanc Regt
154 Inf Bde.

Hour, Date, Place	Summary of Events and Information	Remarks and references to Appendices
September 4th	B Coy from POSTE LESDOS relieved C Coy in the firing line A & D Coys remained in the same places as the previous week.	
5	The enemy shelled our trenches fairly heavily in the morning One shell burst in the midst of a working party killing 1 wounding 5 other ranks of D Coy. Party of 7 returned from leave.	
6 to 10	During this period the men were engaged in deepening the trenches and making artillery shelters & protected look outs. These were for protection in case of heavy bombardment by the enemy. During this time we had	

Army Form C. 2118.

1/4 K.N. Lanc Regt.
154 Inf. Bde.

WAR DIARY
or
INTELLIGENCE SUMMARY
(Erase heading not required.)

Hour, Date, Place	Summary of Events and Information	Remarks and references to Appendices
Sept.		
11.	The 12th Bn. MIDDLESEX. attached for instruction.	
	The battalion was relieved by the 2/5th Lancs Fusrs. about 10 p.m. We then went to POSTE DONNET where C & B Coys. relieved 1 Coy of 1/8th LIVERPOOL IRISH in the front line and A & D Coys remained in support at POSTE DONNET. Lt. Colonel R. HINDLE was in Command of Sector F1.	
14.	1 Other rank Killed. 3 other ranks wounded.	

1247 W 3299 200,000 (E) 8/14 J.B.C. & A. Forms/C. 2118/11.

WAR DIARY
or
INTELLIGENCE SUMMARY

(Erase heading not required.)

Army Form C. 2118.

Instructions regarding War Diaries and Intelligence Summaries are contained in F. S. Regs., Part II. and the Staff Manual respectively. Title pages will be prepared in manuscript.

Hour, Date, Place	Summary of Events and Information	Remarks and references to Appendices
Sept 17	Lt. Colonel F.W. FOLEY left the battalion went to England to take over command of a third line unit.	
18	The battalion was relieved about 9 pm by 1/8th LIVERPOOL IRISH. Just before relief our trenches were heavily shelled. We had the misfortune of losing 1 Coy Sgt. Major, 1 Sgt. & 1 Cpl. with the same shell. 3 O.R's wounded. The Coy's marched independently on being relieved into billets in AVELUY where we took over from 1/6th SCOTTISH RIFLES. The necessary road guards were furnished earlier in the day.	

Army Form C. 2118.

1/4 K.N. Lanc Regt
154 Inf. Bde.

WAR DIARY
or
INTELLIGENCE SUMMARY
(Erase heading not required.)

Instructions regarding War Diaries and Intelligence Summaries are contained in F. S. Regs., Part II. and the Staff Manual respectively. Title pages will be prepared in manuscript.

Hour, Date, Place	Summary of Events and Information	Remarks and references to Appendices
September AVELUY 19	The men were given a rest. No working parties were required except a party consisting of 1 N.C.O. & 20 men to unload R.E. stores. Two voluntary church parades were held. A & B Coys at 6 p.m. C & D Coys at 6-30 p.m. 1 man wounded by stray bullet.	
20	The whole battalion was required for working parties with the exception of D Coy which was inlying picquet.	
21	The 154 Inf. Bde. was relieved by the 153rd Bde. in the evening, and went into billets for a few days rest and training. We were relieved by 1/6th ARGYLL & SUTHERLAND HIGHLANDERS. The relief commenced about 6·15 p.m — as each platoon was relieved	See Operation Order No 17 by Brigadier General G.L. HIBBERT 154 Inf. Bde.

WAR DIARY
or
INTELLIGENCE SUMMARY

(Erase heading not required.)

Army Form C. 2118.

1/4 L.N. Lanc. Regt.
154 Inf. Bde.

Hour, Date, Place	Summary of Events and Information	Remarks and references to Appendices

they marched independently to the new billets in MARTINSART. The whole battalion was settled in about 8 p.m.

Tea food was served out to the men an hour had been eaten earlier than usual.

Our Quartermaster's Store & transport lines which had remained in MARTINSART ever since taking over from the French, were split up.

Q.M Store with 20 mules therefore moved to BOUZINCOURT while the rest of the transport was taken back to VADENCOURT WOOD which is about 10 miles back.

The road guards relieved the 1/6th SCOTTISH RIFLES in MARTINSART about 5-30 p.m.

2/Lt. D. H. OSTREHAN took over the transport in place of 9/Lt HARRIS (to hospital).

Army Form C. 2118.

1/4th K.N. Lanc Regt.
154th Inf Bde.

WAR DIARY
or
INTELLIGENCE SUMMARY
(Erase heading not required.)

Hour, Date, Place	Summary of Events and Information	Remarks and references to Appendices
September 22. MARTINSART	Hours of parade 9-12 & 1 hour in the afternoon under Company arrangements. The morning parade consisted of :- (a) General clean up. (b) Inspection of kits and annexment for stowing all useful articles which could not be carried in the case of an advance. (c) Physical drill. Afternoon parade was devoted to close order drill. ~~Hours parade consisted of physical~~ ~~close order drill~~ Orders were received from 153rd Brigade that the battalion would have to garrison AUTHUILLE.	
11 a.m.	The C.O & Adjutant visited AUTHUILLE in the afternoon made the necessary arrangements.	

WAR DIARY
or
INTELLIGENCE SUMMARY
(Erase heading not required.)

Army Form C. 2118.

1/4th L.N. Lanc
154 Inf Bde.

Hour, Date, Place	Summary of Events and Information	Remarks and references to Appendices
September 22	with 1/6th ROYAL HIGHLANDERS (Black Watch.) The reason for this garrison of AUTHUILLE was as follows. The 1/6th ROYAL HIGHLANDERS were relieving the 1/7th GORDONS in the fire trench, but the latter before coming into billets had to find working parties for AUTHUILLE. As AUTHUILLE could not be left without a garrison we found the necessary number of men. Four guides led the battalion by companies at about 200 yds interval from MARTINSART to AUTHUILLE via BOIS D'AVELUY & everybody were settled in about 9 p.m.	
6-30 p.m.		
23 4-30 a.m.	The 1/7th GORDONS began to arrive & an companies were relieved they march back to MARTINSART where breakfasts were awaiting them. The men were allowed to sleep until dinner time	

Army Form C. 2118.

WAR DIARY
or
INTELLIGENCE SUMMARY
(Erase heading not required.)

1/4 L.N. Lanc Regt;
154 Inf: Bde.

Hour, Date, Place	Summary of Events and Information	Remarks and references to Appendices
Sept. 23	A Company were the last to arrive in MARTINSART. They were in a place called the MOUND KEEP about 1/2 mile from AUTHUILLE. On relief they had to take up R.E stores to the fire trench.	
7 p.m	Heavy rain fell accompanied by a great deal of lightning & this continued throughout the night.	
24.	Companies went a Route March following one another at 1/4 hour intervals. The first company timed to start at 9.a.m but heavy rain was falling & it was postponed. The first Company eventually left at 9-30am The route taken was. ENGELBELMER, POINT 97, HEDAUVILLE, BOUZINCOURT track to MARTINSART via the runaway road. The rain had made the roads very heavy muddy consequently it was heavy going.	Reference map AMIENS 12.

WAR DIARY
or
INTELLIGENCE SUMMARY
(Erase heading not required.)

Army Form C. 2118.

1/4 L.N. Lanc. Regt.
154 Inf: Bde

Hour, Date, Place	Summary of Events and Information	Remarks and references to Appendices
September 24. 5-30 pm.	The chemical adviser to 3rd Army lectured the battalion on the use & care of Smoke Helmets. A number of men passed through a barn which was filled with the gas.	
25.	Companies carried out training in close order drill, bayonet fighting, physical drill etc.	
6 pm	Orders were received that the 154th Inf Bde would relieve 152nd Inf Bde on night 26-27 Sept.	See Operation Order 18 by Brig: General G.L. HIBBERT
26.	Billeting officer went to AVELUY. arranged for billets. These were exactly the same as the ones vacated by us on Sept. 21st. We took over the road guards in AVELUY about 4 p.m. The battalion moved out from MARTINSART in half companies at 5 min. interval C Coy starting about 4 p.m.	

Army Form C. 2118.

1/4 L.N. Lanc Reg.t
154 Inf Bde

WAR DIARY
or
INTELLIGENCE SUMMARY.
(Erase heading not required.)

Place	Date	Hour	Summary of Events and Information	Remarks and references to Appendices
	Sept. 26.	5.45.	The move was completed. The men had tea on arrival.	
	27.		A few R.E. fatigues had to be found. Companies carried on training.	
			Capt. H. PARKER. ⎫	
			Capt. J.A. CRUMP. ⎬ rejoined the battalion from	
			Lieut. K.H. MOORE. ⎬ 3/4th L.N. Lanc Reg.t	
			Lieut. R. ORD ⎬	
			Lieut. J.L. BRINDLE. ⎭	
			Capt. PARKER took over command of A Coy	
			" CRUMP " " " B "	
			Lieut ORD " " " D Coy.	
			Lieut MOORE posted to A Coy & Lieut BRINDLE to C Coy.	
	28		The whole battalion with exception of its inlying picquet	

Army Form C. 2118.

1/4 L.N. Lanc Regt.
154 Inf: Bde.

WAR DIARY
or
INTELLIGENCE SUMMARY.
(Erase heading not required.)

Instructions regarding War Diaries and Intelligence Summaries are contained in F. S. Regs., Part II and the Staff Manual respectively. Title pages will be prepared in manuscript.

Place	Date	Hour	Summary of Events and Information	Remarks and references to Appendices
	Sept.		- picquet -	
	28.		was employed on working parties etc. A very successful concert was held in the evening.	
	29.		Battalion again on working parties.	
	30.		Same as 29th. Weather very cold. Bathing place for hot baths started in MELUX.	

1577 Wt.W10791/1773 500,000 1/15 D. D. & L. A.D.S.S./Forms/C. 2118.

51st Division

121/7470

CONFIDENTIAL

WAR DIARY

OF:

1/4th Battalion the Loyal North Lancashire Regiment.

From 1st October 1915. To 31st October 1915.

Vol III

Army Form C. 2118.

WAR DIARY
or
INTELLIGENCE SUMMARY.
(Erase heading not required.)

1/4th L.N. Lanc Regt
154 Inf. Bde.

Place	Date	Hour	Summary of Events and Information	Remarks and references to Appendices
ANFROY.	Oct 1.		The usual working parties were required which absorbed the whole battalion with the exception of the in lying picquet. The enemy put two shells into the village about 8 a.m. & again two more in the evening without however doing any damage. Brigadier General G.L. HIBBERT was wounded in the shoulder in the afternoon and Lt. Colonel R. HINDLE took over temporary command of the 154 Inf Brigade. Major H. NICKSON took over command of the Battalion with Capt. J. CRUMP as second in command. The weather is getting very cold & there was quite a heavy frost at night. Capt. REINNARD & 2/Lt NORWOOD went to hospital.	
	2.	8 a.m	Orders were received to go into the trenches on Oct 3rd. Major NICKSON & Company Commanders went up to the	

Army Form C. 2118.

1/4 L.N. Lanc Regt
154 Inf Bde

WAR DIARY
or
INTELLIGENCE SUMMARY.
(Erase heading not required.)

Place	Date	Hour	Summary of Events and Information	Remarks and references to Appendices
	OCT			
	2		trenches in the afternoon. The 1/6th SCOTTISH RIFLES & 1/4th N. Lanc Regt were to take over F2 sector which we had held before. It was decided to put the companies in the same places as formerly.	
	3	2 p.m.	The first platoon & headquarters left AVELUY for the trenches. This was the first occasion on which a relief by daylight had been tried, the result being very satisfactory. Guides were dispensed with, & the companies were settled in the trenches much quicker than usual. Companies left AVELUY in the following order by platoons with 1/4 hour interval between companies A. C. & D coys - were in the firing line. B coy in Support at POSTE LESBOS. Relief completed at 4 p.m.	

Army Form C. 2118.

WAR DIARY
or
INTELLIGENCE SUMMARY.
(Erase heading not required.)

1/4 L.N. Lanc Regt.
15th Inf Bde

Place	Date	Hour	Summary of Events and Information	Remarks and references to Appendices
	OCT			
	3		1/6th SCOTTISH RIFLES were on our left & 1/3rd LIVERPOOL IRISH on our right in F1 Sector. 1 man wounded. Capt. GREGSON to hospital.	
	4		Nothing unusual to report. A flare which dropped into enemy's trench set fire to some material which blazed furiously. Capt. GREEN R.A.M.C. reported for duty vice Lieut Syano who was transferred to the 3rd Division. 1 O.R. wounded	
	5	11pm	An observation post was discovered from which German ration parties could be observed. A machine gun was trained on the place & by firing single shots at least four of the enemy were put out of action. The range was about 950 yds.	

Army Form C. 2118.

1/4 L.N. Lanc Reg.
154 Inf Bde

WAR DIARY
or
INTELLIGENCE SUMMARY.
(Erase heading not required.)

Place	Date	Hour	Summary of Events and Information	Remarks and references to Appendices
TRENCHES	Oct			
	5		16 ORs joined the battalion from the Base. 1 OR wounded.	
			Orders were issued to keep a special look out for the enemy going back. It seemed to be the opinion that they would withdraw from this section of the line if the advance of the British & French succeeded.	
	6		Howitzers were laid on enemy machine gun emplacements which had been located the previous night. The M.Gs opened fire at dusk but were immediately silenced	
	7		Nothing unusual to report. Brigadier General G.T.G. EDWARDS. C.B. took over command of the 154th Inf: Bde: Lt Colonel R. HINDLE rejoined the battalion.	

WAR DIARY
or
INTELLIGENCE SUMMARY.

(Erase heading not required.)

Lt L. N. Kane Regt.
15th Inf. Bgde.

Army Form C. 2118.

Place	Date	Hour	Summary of Events and Information	Remarks and references to Appendices
	Oct. 8.		Lt. STRONG and other rank went to WISQUES for a machine gun course.	
	9.	5.30pm 6.45pm	Unusually quiet day. Sounds were heard on POZIERS – THIEPVAL road as if proceeding from an armoured car. One O.R. wounded.	
	10		Our howitzers silenced enemy trench mortar at point A.12. Enemy very "jumpy" throughout the night sending up an unusually large number of flares. An officers patrol under Lt NOLAN discovered a big oval shaped hole near point A.12. The hole was about 20 feet long & 10 deep was approached by a safe running beneath the enemy's wire.	Trench Plan direction Sparrow

Army Form C. 2118.

Lt. L.N. Kerr Sgt.
154 Inf Bde.

WAR DIARY
or
INTELLIGENCE SUMMARY.
(Erase heading not required.)

Place	Date	Hour	Summary of Events and Information	Remarks and references to Appendices
	Oct			
	11.		Enemy's "work" mentioned on 10th could not be seen as it was cleverly hidden by the contour of the ground. Our Howitzers registered the point without getting a direct hit. Have commenced again.	
	12.	6.30p	The work at 4P again reconnoitred was found to be occupied.	
		11p.m	2 Enemy searchlights were seen in the direction of BAPAUME an aeroplane was heard over our lines. One O.R. wounded	
	13.		Observation of enemy's "work" found to be roofed in covered with a layer of cinders. Enemy more active than usual probably initiated by our howitzer fire.	

Army Form C. 2118.

1/4 L.N. Lanc Regt.
154 Inf. Bde.

WAR DIARY
or
INTELLIGENCE SUMMARY.
(Erase heading not required.)

Instructions regarding War Diaries and Intelligence Summaries are contained in F.S. Regs., Part II. and the Staff Manual respectively. Title pages will be prepared in manuscript.

Place	Date	Hour	Summary of Events and Information	Remarks and references to Appendices
	Oct			
	14		Nothing unusual to report.	
	15		The battalion was relieved by 4/5th LANCS FUSRS. & proceeded to F.1 sector. B&C Coy's relieved one company 1/8th LIVERPOOL IRISH on the extreme right of the sector A&D Coy's remained in support at POSTE DONNET. Relief completed at 3-45 p.m. 1/4th ROYAL LANCASTER regt. remained of the sector the 53rd Brigade 18th Division troops are on our right. One O.R. wounded.	
	16		Exceedingly quiet.	
	17		Very quiet on F sector front. A heavy bombardment was heard some miles to our left, which continued all day.	

1577 Wt.W10791/1773 500,000 1/15 D.D.&L. A.D.S.S./Forms/C. 2118.

Army Form C. 2118.

WAR DIARY
or
INTELLIGENCE SUMMARY.
(Erase heading not required.)

1/4 L.N. Lanc Regt
154 Inf. Bde.

Place	Date	Hour	Summary of Events and Information	Remarks and references to Appendices
	Oct			
	18		Work was commenced on the new shelter in F Sector. Most of the existing shelters are very weak & quite inadequate. This battalion found parties 2-5 each consisting of 1NCO+6 men. Parties worked in 4 hour shifts.	
		6-30-11pm	D Coy. wiring CONISTON ST.	
		11-15pm	Word came from Brigade that there were indications that the enemy might deliver a gas attack on 3rd Army front. Everybody warned & orders were issued to keep a special vigilance. 1 O.R. wounded.	
	19.		Work on shelter was increased to 3 reliefs. 1st & 2nd reliefs found by us commenced work at 5-30 & 9-30 a.m respectively. 3rd relief was found from another Brigade. Hot tea & extra rations were issued to the men who started work at 5-30 a.m.	

WAR DIARY
or
INTELLIGENCE SUMMARY.

Army Form C. 2118.

1/4th L.N. Lanc Regt.
154 Inf: Bde.

Place	Date	Hour	Summary of Events and Information	Remarks and references to Appendices
	Oct			
	19.		Orders were received to keep a special look out for any change in enemy's troops.	
		6-10pm	"A" Coy continued wiring of CONISTON ST. 1 O.R. wounded.	
	20		Working parties same as for 19th inst.	
	21		Working parties same as for 20th inst. The battalion was relieved in the fire trench by two companies of 1/8th LIVERPOOL IRISH, & in the rear trench by "C" "D" companies 1/4th ROYAL LANCASTERS, and proceeded to billets in AVELUY. The relief was completed at 3.30 p.m. Brigade HQ 2 O.R. wounded.	
AVELUY	22.		Working parties required which absorbed "A" "C" "D" companies. "B" Company had the battery horses allotted to them. In accordance with instructions from Brigade Headquarters, the first stage of the T.A.C. alarm was practised, and Orders in case of attack. The Brigadier inspected "B" Company, which was standing to outside its Headquarters. Scouts PO	

Army Form C. 2118.

1/4 L. N. Lanc Regt
154 Inf. Bde.

WAR DIARY
or
INTELLIGENCE SUMMARY.
(Erase heading not required.)

Instructions regarding War Diaries and Intelligence Summaries are contained in F.S. Regs., Part II. and the Staff Manual respectively. Title pages will be prepared in manuscript.

Place	Date	Hour	Summary of Events and Information	Remarks and references to Appendices
AVELUY	Oct			
	23.		Working parties absorbed A, B & D Companies. These ceased, with one exception, at noon, so that the T.A.C. alarm might be practised in its entirety. At 3.13 p.m. the T.A.C. was received from Brigade Headquarters, and at 3.45 p.m. the Battalion was reported complete in its attack quarters, & was inspected later by the Brigadier.	
	24		Working parties absorbed most of A, B & C Companies. D Company bathed. Church of England Church parade was held for available men at 11 a.m. on the Brigade Grenade School ground.	
	25		Working parties absorbed bulk of 3 Companies. The other company bathed. A draft of 67 men arrived from the 3/4 L.N.L. Regt. and was distributed to companies A 15, B 12, C 22, D 18, bringing all companies approximately to the same strength of rifles available for the fire trench.	
	26		Orders were received to relieve the 2/5 Lancs. Fus. tomorrow at K55 00 S on F2 Sketch.	

WAR DIARY
or
INTELLIGENCE SUMMARY.

(Erase heading not required.)

1/4 1/5 L.N Lan Army Form C. 2118.
154 Inf Bde

Place	Date	Hour	Summary of Events and Information	Remarks and references to Appendices
ANZUY	Oct 26		Working parties absorbed 3 companies.	
	27	1.30pm	Fur coats were issued to the battalion. The first platoon Headquarters left for the trenches. The remainder of the battalion followed & the relief was completed at 3.16 p.m. A, C, D companies in the fire trench B company in support at POSTE LESDOS	
	28		1/6 R. SCOTTISH RIFLES (Lt. Col. KAY in charge of F2 sector) on our left & 1/8 R. LIVERPOOL IRISH on our right in F1 sector.	
	29		Enemy bombarded the wire & fire trench along the front held by our 3 companies between 7.10 a.m. and 9.30 a.m. Considerable damage was done to the wire in front of the wood held by "C" Company, and the trench in the same place was blown in for about 100 yards between AINTREE ST and MERSEY ST. About 30 yards of parapet was badly damaged in "A" Company's section immediately	

WAR DIARY or INTELLIGENCE SUMMARY

Army Form C. 2118.

4th L.N. Lanc Regt.
154 3rd Bde

Place	Date	Hour	Summary of Events and Information	Remarks and references to Appendices
North of AINTREE ST.	29		During the day parties were engaged in clearing the trench, including a party of 1 Officer + 20 O.R. from 4 KORL Regt from the Brigade Reserve. At 7 pm a party of 3 officers and 133 men from the 1/4th KORL Regt arrived + worked until 5 am on the wire and parapet. The garrison was withdrawn from the damaged section of the "wood trench" and used to thicken the flanks, while 1 Officer + 40 O.R. of the Reserve company were taken up and posted in support of "C" Company in the communication trench running N. and S. behind the damaged section.	
		7pm		
	29/30	12 mid	"A" Company reported their parapet on a fair state of repair. The desultory shelling of the working party continued. Salvos of H.E. A.V. shells were sent over about hourly. MAJOR H. NICKSON being killed during one of these bursts. SEC. LIEUT. A.B. BRATION and 6 Ok Ranks wounded.	
	30		Work was continued all day on the damaged trench. A considerable amount of rifle + machine gun fire was reported from the enemy. A party of 3 Officers and	

Army Form C. 2118.

1/4th L.N. Lane Regt
154 Inf. Bde

WAR DIARY
or
INTELLIGENCE SUMMARY.
(Erase heading not required.)

Instructions regarding War Diaries and Intelligence Summaries are contained in F.S. Regs., Part II. and the Staff Manual respectively. Title pages will be prepared in manuscript.

Place	Date	Hour	Summary of Events and Information	Remarks and references to Appendices
	Oct.			
	30	8pm	100 other ranks of 1/4 K.O.R.L. Regt reported at 8pm and worked till about 12.30 a.m. on the damaged trench and wire. Enemy artillery & machine guns were more active than on the preceding night. The supporting company remained at POSTE LES DOS during the night. There were a few casualties (1 O.R. killed, 2 O.R. wounded) among the KINGS OWN working party during the night. MAJOR H. NICKSON killed, 5 O.R. wounded, 1 O.R. missing.	
	31		Comparatively quiet day. A party of 3 officers & 60 O.R. 8th ROYAL SCOTS arrived to repair damage to wire & trench in the wood and were billeted partly in the reserve shelters at LES DOS near the cookers & partly in the shelters near the 6 SCOTTISH RIFLES headquarters. CAPT. J.O. WIDDOWS went to F. Ambulance sick. 2Lt M.H. NOBLAN & 2 O.R. wounded.	

R. Hindle. Lieut/Colonel
1/4 L.N. Lane Regt

51/5 Brown

1/7rd Royal N⁺ᵈ Lancs. Rgt.
1/4⁺ʰ —
Vol IV

131/7694

WAR DIARY

OF

1/4th "LOYAL" NORTH LANCASHIRE REGIMENT.

From 1st November 1915.

To 30th November 1915.

Army Form C. 2118.

WAR DIARY
or
INTELLIGENCE SUMMARY.
(Erase heading not required.)

Place	Date	Hour	Summary of Events and Information	Remarks and references to Appendices
LESDOS	Nov 1		During the night army was proceeded with by the ROYAL SCOTS. Fairly quiet night to-day. Salvos of 77 m.m shells were fired by the enemy at frequent intervals with little apparent result. 1 O.R. wounded. 7 O.R. to H.F.A.	
	2		2/Lt. R.S. DE BLABY reported for duty from the base. Usual working parties on artillery shelters front line trenches. The ROYAL SCOTS continued the wiring at night. B Company relieved C Company in the front line the latter proceeding to reserve at POST LESDOS. Lt. has rained fell all day. The trenches in several places were badly damaged parts of the "parados" (parapet falling in. The trenches were very soon three deep in water much the sumps (for drainage) soon becoming full. 3 O.R. to H.F.A.	

WAR DIARY
or
INTELLIGENCE SUMMARY.
(Erase heading not required.)

Army Form C. 2118.

1/4th L. N. Lanc. Regt.
154 Inf. Bde.

Place	Date	Hour	Summary of Events and Information	Remarks and references to Appendices
LES·DOS	Nov 3		Usual working parties. Fairly quiet day. One enemy shell which burst in the French Wed by A Company killed two men wounded one while three others were admitted to hospital suffering from shock. The trenches are free of mud & the men are very wet. 2 O.R. killed. 1 O.R. wounded. 11 O.R. to F.A.	
	4		Two extra parties from ARGYLL & SUTHERLAND HIGHLANDERS were engaged in draining communication trenches. All work was stopped at 1 p.m. as the artillery were doing an unusual amount of firing in the afternoon & retaliation by the enemy was expected.	

Army Form C. 2118.

1/4th L.N Lancs Regt.
154 Inf. Bde.

WAR DIARY
or
INTELLIGENCE SUMMARY.

(Erase heading not required.)

Place	Date	Hour	Summary of Events and Information	Remarks and references to Appendices
LESDOS.	Nov 4		The fire from fried about 70 rounds, the bombers about 80. Fire was chiefly directed on the German Sap H24 also on their trenches, at H11 T4h2. Several direct hits were obtained + a good deal of their wire was cut. During the night many working parties were heard mending them were fired on by our artillery with very satisfactory results. 1 O.R. to H.F.A.	
	5		Usual working parties. The day passed very quietly.	
		10 p.m	About 11 p.m the enemy sent over two landed at the junction of Austin Street the fire trench. 3 men were killed + 3 wounded shells which who were waiting as sentry reliefs. Owing to the number of sick + wounded it is becoming	

Army Form C. 2118.

WAR DIARY
or
INTELLIGENCE SUMMARY.
(Erase heading not required.)

1/4th L.N. Lanc. Regt.
154th Inf. Bde

Place	Date	Hour	Summary of Events and Information	Remarks and references to Appendices
LESDOS	Nov 5		more difficult every day to find the requisite number of men for the different duties. 3 O.R. killed 3 O.R. wounded 6 O.R. to H.F.A. Lt. Colonel R. HINDLE went on leave. Capt. CRUMP taking over command.	
	6		Working parties as usual. The day passed very quietly. On the night of 6/7 the 1st Aberdeen battery pulled up a gun into the forward area, intending to fire at dawn. The gun was situated at the junction of CONISTON St. & the wood but owing to a "relief" on the 7th inst. it was deemed inadvisable to fire & the gun was taken back to the battery. 7 O.R. to H.F.A.	
	7	8 a.m.	Word was received that the 154th Inf: Bde would be relieved by 152nd Inf: Bde. in the course of the afternoon.	

Army Form C. 2118.

1/4th L.N. Lanc Regt.
154 Inf. Bde.

WAR DIARY
or
INTELLIGENCE SUMMARY.
(Erase heading not required.)

Instructions regarding War Diaries and Intelligence Summaries are contained in F. S. Regs., Part II. and the Staff Manual respectively. Title pages will be prepared in manuscript.

Place	Date	Hour	Summary of Events and Information	Remarks and references to Appendices
	Nov 7		The C.O. & O.C. Coy.s 1/5th SEAFORTH'S arrived about 12 noon to look over the trenches. 16 guides under an officer from the fire trench & 8 guides under an officer from Coy.s in reserve met the relieving battalion at the 10 barrier in AVELUY about 3-15 p.m. The relief was successfully carried out & finished about 6 p.m. The battalion marched by 1/2 Companies to BOUZINCOURT where Lt. MOORE had obtained billets. The last company arrived about 9-30 p.m. 1 O.R. to H.F.A.	via main road from AVELUY
BOUZINCOURT	8.		The battalion was allowed to rest for the men to clean clothing equipment etc. All officers with exception of 1 per Coy attended at Bde.	

Army Form C. 2118.

WAR DIARY
or
INTELLIGENCE SUMMARY.
(Erase heading not required.)

1/4th L.N. Lanc. Regt.
154th Inf. Bde.

Place	Date	Hour	Summary of Events and Information	Remarks and references to Appendices
	Nov			
BOUZINCOURT	8		Headquarters where Colonel IAN STUART lectured to the Brigade officers on "the attack". 2 O.R. to H.F.A.	
	9.		The day was devoted to infantries efficiency & in kit made up. Very heavy rain fell all at night. 2 O.R. to H.F.A.	
	10.		Companies carried out training according to programme. which consisted of Physical drill. – Close order drill. – bayonet fighting etc. – A football match was arranged with 1/4th KING'S OWN at HENNENCOURT but it was scratched owing to rain. Hours of parade 9 – 12. The afternoons men have to themselves for games etc.	

WAR DIARY
or
INTELLIGENCE SUMMARY.

Army Form C. 2118.

1/4th K.N.Lane Regt.
154 Inf: Bde.

Place	Date	Hour	Summary of Events and Information	Remarks and references to Appendices
BOUZINCOURT	Nov 11		We had to find 7 Officers & 300 other ranks for working parties in G & F Sectors, the two parties in G. sector left BOUZINCOURT at 6.30 a.m. the remaining parties for F sector leaving at 7. a.m. Tea rations been taken, dinners being eaten on return to billets. All work ceased at 2.30 p.m. 2 O.R. to H.F.A.	
	12.		The programme of training was not adhered to owing to the wet weather. Companies carried on with lectures in billets. 5 O.R. to H.F.A.	
	13.		The battalion carried out an attack on the dummy trenches outside BOUZINCOURT in accordance with Colonel IAN STUART'S lecture of 8th inst.	

WAR DIARY
or
INTELLIGENCE SUMMARY.

Army Form C. 2118.

1/4th L.N. Lanc. Regt.
154 Inf. Bde.

Place	Date	Hour	Summary of Events and Information	Remarks and references to Appendices
BUZINCOURT	13		The morning was very "bluely" wet. The Adjutant & Commanding officer attended a conference at Bde. H.Q. 3 OR to H.F.A.	
	14		The battalion received orders that we should go into AUTHUILLE on Nov. 16. The C.O. Adjt. Q.M. & O.C. Coys proceeded there to look round the village. Early Communion was celebrated at 7.30 a.m. in the 1/6th SEAFORTH'S Canteen. A voluntary service was held in C Coy.'s billets at 6.30 p.m. Colonel HINDLE returned from leave. 2 OR to H.F.A.	

Army Form C. 2118.

1/4th L.N. Lanc Regt.
154 Inf. Bde.

WAR DIARY
or
INTELLIGENCE SUMMARY.
(Erase heading not required.)

Place	Date	Hour	Summary of Events and Information	Remarks and references to Appendices
BOUZINCOURT	Nov 15		The Brigadier should have inspected the Battalion in "the attack" but this was cancelled owing to the battalion having to find working parties of 300 men. Snow fell during the early hours of the morning. 1 O.R. killed 5 to H.F.A. 1 to Base for discharge.	
	16.		More snow fell. The Battalion left BOUZINCOURT for AUTHUILLE by 1/2 Companies meeting the guides of 1/6th GORDON's at the barrier S' end of AUTHUILLE at 7.30 p.m. Relief was completed at 8.20 p.m. D Coy at MOUND KEEP. A " in centre of the village. B " BLACK HORSE ROAD C " along AUTHUILLE — AVELUY ROAD. From BOUZINCOURT the battalion marched via the main road to AVELUY thence to AUTHUILLE along road E of RIVER L'ANCRE	Operation Order No 20 by Brigadier General G.T.G. EDWARDS C.B.

Army Form C. 2118.

1/4th L.N. Lanc. Regt.
154 Inf. Bde.

WAR DIARY
or
INTELLIGENCE SUMMARY.
(Erase heading not required.)

Place	Date	Hour	Summary of Events and Information	Remarks and references to Appendices
	Nov			
	16.		Some of the shelters - especially in B company are in a very bad state of repair. Very little fire was noticed from the front line trenches. Officer reinforcements 2/Lt T.A. BURNSIDE. 2/Lt J.R. BEST. 2/Lt R.M. WILSON. 6 OR to H.F.A.	
	17.	11 a.m.	The Battalion found working parties for 165 N.C.O's men. 13 officers. The remainder of the men were engaged in repairing their own shelters. The enemy put about 20 shells into the village without doing much damage. 1 OR wounded.	
	18.		4 working parties were employed under the R.E. All other available men under Capt. PARKER were employed	

Army Form C. 2118.

1/4th L.N. Lanc Regt.
154 Inf. Bde.

WAR DIARY
or
INTELLIGENCE SUMMARY.
(Erase heading not required.)

Place	Date	Hour	Summary of Events and Information	Remarks and references to Appendices
AUTHUILLE	Nov 18		On a support trench in G1 sub-section. The day passed very quietly. The weather was damp & misty.	
	19.		Working parties same as for 18th. Another very quiet day. 3 OR to H.F.A.	
	20		Our artillery had a "shoot" against the German trenches about 2.30 p.m. the enemy replied with about 30 smoke shells on AUTHUILLE. 1 man was killed otherwise no damage was done. 1 OR killed 5 to H.F.A.	
	21.		Usual working parties. Nothing of interest to record. 5 OR to H.F.A.	

WAR DIARY
or
INTELLIGENCE SUMMARY.
(Erase heading not required.)

Army Form C. 2118.

1/4th L.N. Lanc. Reg.t
154 Inf.y Bde.

Place	Date	Hour	Summary of Events and Information	Remarks and references to Appendices
	Nov			
	22	9 a.m.	Word was received that we should relieve the 1/4th R.L. Reg.t in sub-section G1A. during the course of the afternoon. Company officers visited the lines during the morning. At 2-30 p.m. the relief commenced & was completed at 3-45 p.m. Order of companies from right to left in the fire trench was D, B, C. with A company in support. The trenches are in a very bad state of repair & a big amount of work is required on them. Shelter accomodation is poor. During the period the B.H.Q. was in AUTHUILLE the weather was fine but very misty cold with frost at night.	
	23.		Quiet day. 4 O.Rs to H.F.A	
	24.		The Brigade organised a "fire scheme" against the German trenches, with the idea of making the enemy disclose	

Army Form C. 2118.

1/4th L.N. Lanc. Regt.
167 Inf. Bde.

WAR DIARY
or
INTELLIGENCE SUMMARY.
(Erase heading not required.)

Place	Date	Hour	Summary of Events and Information	Remarks and references to Appendices
TRENCHES	Nov 24		his trench positions. Our trench mortars, "West Bomb Throwers" & rifle grenadiers bombarded the enemy front line trenches which induced the enemy to reply with two heavy mortars. The position of these was communicated to the artillery who bombarded them with Howitzers field gun with very good effect. The enemy replied with about 30 small shells on AUTHUILLE without damage. The fired lasted about 2½ hours commencing at 10 a.m. During this time all men, with exception of sentries, were under cover in artillery shelters. All work was suspended. The remainder of the day passed quietly. 1 OR to H.F.A.	
	25.	2a.m	The day was quiet with the exception of a little shelling on both sides. Pounder GENT (D Coy) did very good work taking 9 bombs with him he set out on his own reconnoitering	

Army Form C. 2118.

WAR DIARY
or
INTELLIGENCE SUMMARY.
(Erase heading not required.)

1/4th L.N. Lanc. Regt.
154 Inf. Bde.

Place	Date	Hour	Summary of Events and Information	Remarks and references to Appendices
TRENCHES.	Nov. 25		An enemy patrol coming from a Saphead, bombed them with good effect. 1 OR killed 3 ORs to H.F.A.	
	26		Another fire scheme was initiated with the object of cutting enemy wire & causing casualties by machine guns when they came out to repair it at night. M.G.s kept up bursts of indirect fire throughout the following night on those portions of wire which had been cut. About noon enemy replied fully with field gun on front line trenches & AUTHUILLE. 2/Lieut K.H. MOORE was killed by a sniper.	
	27	8.30am	Enemy M.G fire practically nil. 2 ORs to H.F.A.	

Army Form C. 2118.

1/4th L.N. Lanc. Regt.
154 Inf. Bde.

WAR DIARY
or
INTELLIGENCE SUMMARY.
(Erase heading not required.)

Instructions regarding War Diaries and Intelligence Summaries are contained in F. S. Regs., Part II. and the Staff Manual respectively. Title pages will be prepared in manuscript.

Place	Date	Hour	Summary of Events and Information	Remarks and references to Appendices
TRENCHES	Nov 28		Brigade was relieved by 152nd Brigade. 1/9th ARGYLL & SUTHERLAND Hdrs relieved our Batt; in G1 sub-sector. Relief was completed about 7-45 p.m & companies reached billets in BOUZINCOURT about 9-30 p.m. During the last 6 days in the trenches the weather has been fine & frosty.	Operation Order No 21 by BgdrGen G.T.G. EDWARDS 154 Bde.
BOUZINCOURT	29		Day occupied in inspections & cleaning up. Day was very wet.	
			Historical tactics for recent training 10R to H.F.A.	
	30		Company training 10R to H.F.A.	

WAR DIARY.

OF

THE 1/4TH LOYAL NORTH LANCASHIRE REGIMENT.

55

FROM 1ST DECEMBER 1915.

TO 31ST DECEMBER 1915.

Vol V

Army Form C. 2118.

1/4th L.N. Lanc. Reg.
154 Inf. Bde

WAR DIARY
OF
INTELLIGENCE SUMMARY.
(Erase heading not required.)

Instructions regarding War Diaries and Intelligence Summaries are contained in F.S. Regs., Part II and the Staff Manual respectively. Title pages will be prepared in manuscript.

Place	Date	Hour	Summary of Events and Information	Remarks and references to Appendices
BOUZINCOURT	1.		The whole battalion was engaged on working parties. The 17th H.L.I. arrived in the village and were billeted in tents which our men had erected the previous day. 1 OTR to H.F.A.	
	2.		The battalion spent the morning in practicing the attack which the Brigadier witnessed. Afterwards the battalion was drawn up & S.Q.M.S. E.E. LESTER was presented with the "Croix de Guerre" for conspicuous bravery at FESTUBERT June 15/16.	
	3.		Company training. About 7 p.m. a test alarm was sent out, companies were ready to move in twenty minutes. 4 ORs to H.F.A.	

Army Form C. 2118.

WAR DIARY
or
INTELLIGENCE SUMMARY.
(Erase heading not required.)

1/4th N. Lanc. Reg.t
154 Inf. Bde.

Place	Date	Hour	Summary of Events and Information	Remarks and references to Appendices
BOUZINCOURT	Dec 4		The day was very wet and parades were under Company arrangements which consisted chiefly of lectures. Word was received that we should go into the trenches on 5th. 1 OR to H.F.A.	
	5.		O.C. Coys proceeded to Hd Qrs of 1/6 BLACK WATCH in F2 Sub-Sector to take over trenches, stores, etc. The battalion left BOUZINCOURT at 1 p.m. proceeding via ALBERT & AVELUY by 1/2 Companies at 200x distance. The relief was successfully completed at 5 p.m. though very much slower than usual owing to the muddy state of the trenches. A,B, & C Coys held the firing line from night of F2 AINTREE ST with D Coy in support. The 2/5 Lancs Fuslrs held the remainder of the sector with one company in support at LESBOEUFS. 7 ORs to H.F.A.	See 154/1/ Bde Operation Order 22. by Brig Gen. G.T.G. Edwards

Army Form C. 2118.

1/4 L.N. Lanc. Reg.t
154 Inf. Bde.

WAR DIARY
or
INTELLIGENCE SUMMARY.
(Erase heading not required.)

Place	Date	Hour	Summary of Events and Information	Remarks and references to Appendices
TRENCHES	Dec 6		The night 5/6 passed very quietly. Three companies of 1/4 L.N.Lanc.R. were relieved by 2 Companies (C & D) 17th H.L.I. who were in for instruction. Two officers of 1/4 L.N.Lanc. were left behind (one attached to each company of the H.L.I.) 4 bombers per Coy. The three companies of 1/4 L.N.L. proceeded to billets in AVELUY under command of Capt. GREGSON. The trenches are in a very bad condition and all available men are employed on draining the trenches with pumps, buckets etc. 1 O.R. to H.F.A. 2/Lt. A. HAGUE arrived from 3/4 L.N.Lanc. Regt.	
	7.	3 p.m.	Our artillery commenced a pre-arranged fire scheme but owing to heavy rain it was discontinued as observation	

WAR DIARY
or
INTELLIGENCE SUMMARY.

(Erase heading not required.)

Army Form C. 2118.

1/4 L.N. Lanc. Regt.
154th Inf. Bde.

Place	Date	Hour	Summary of Events and Information	Remarks and references to Appendices
TRENCHES	Dec 7		was impossible. The Germans retaliated with field guns with very little damage. 1 OR 6 H.F.A.	
	8.	2.30pm	The two companies H.L.I were relieved by 3 coys 1/4 L.N. Lanc Regt. The day was fine & good headway was made with drawing etc. 16 OR 6 H.F.A.	
	9.	3.15pm	2 companies 1/6th Scottish Rifles relieved 1 company 2/5th LANCS. FUSLRS. who went into billets in ANEUY. Very heavy rain fell during the night, bringing down several parts of the trenches. 1 OR wounded 1 OR 6 H.F.A.	

Army Form C. 2118.

WAR DIARY
or
INTELLIGENCE SUMMARY.
(Erase heading not required.)

1/4th L.N. Lanc. Regt.
154 Inf. Bde.

Place	Date	Hour	Summary of Events and Information	Remarks and references to Appendices
TRENCHES.	10		Nothing of importance to record.	
	11		"D" Coy relieved "B" Coy in the firing line. Enemy artillery very active about 4 p.m. & between 9 p.m. & 2 a.m. (12th). A large number of shells were fired into AVELUY, MARTINSART, & ALBERT. The day was fine but heavy rain fell at night turning to snow during the early hours of the morning of the 12th. 2 OR to H.F.A.	
	12		Enemy very quiet. Officers & N.C.Os of B Coy 11th BORDER REGT attached to us for instruction. Rain & sleet all day. 3 OR to H.F.A.	

Army Form C. 2118.

WAR DIARY
or
INTELLIGENCE SUMMARY.

(Erase heading not required.)

1/4 L.N. Lanc Regt
154 Inf. Bde.

Place	Date	Hour	Summary of Events and Information	Remarks and references to Appendices
TRENCHES DEC	13th	2 pm	Platoons of "B" Coy 11th BORDER REGT came into the line for instruction. the platoons, they were divided among the four companys front line. Owing to the bad state & the lack of accommodation of shelters an equal number of men were withdrawn to the shelters at CRUCIFIX CORNER. 1 OR. wounded 1 OR. to H.F.A.	
	14th		Platoon of B Coy 11th BORDERS left the line & Officers & N.C.O.s of D Coy (same regiment) came in for instruction. 5 OR. to H.F.A.	
	15th		Platoon of D Coy 11th BORDERS attacked for instruction. these came in about 11 a.m. & our own men were withdrawn the same as for 13th.	
		2 p.m.	A "Fire scheme" commenced in which "Trench Mortars" field guns & Howitzers took part. The idea was to cut the enemy	

WAR DIARY or INTELLIGENCE SUMMARY.

Army Form C. 2118.

1/4 L.N. Lanc Regt.
154 Inf. Bde.

Place	Date	Hour	Summary of Events and Information	Remarks and references to Appendices
	15.		were twenty men casualties by M.G fire while repairing at night. Owing to this had light observation was very difficult & the scheme was not the success that some one had been. The enemy retaliated with mortars & field guns without any material damage being done. 1 R. H.F.A.	
	16.		Platoon of 11th BORDERS were relieved about 10.30 a.m. during the afternoon the 154 Inf Bde was relieved by 152 Inf; Bde. F2 the 1/6th SEAFORTHS relieved the firing line & the 1/5 SEAFORTHS the two companies in reserve at LESBOS. The relief was successfully completed at 5.30 p.m. the battalion reached BOUZINCOURT, where billets had been arranged, about 7 p.m. 1 or G. H.F.A.	See Routine Order No.2 by Brig. General G.T.G. EDWARDS 154 Inf Bde

Army Form C. 2118.

WAR DIARY
or
INTELLIGENCE SUMMARY.
(Erase heading not required.)

1/4 L.N. Lanc Regt.
154 Inf. Bde.

Place	Date	Hour	Summary of Events and Information	Remarks and references to Appendices
BOUZINCOURT	Dec 17		The day was allotted to the men for cleaning clothes, equipment etc also for inspections. 1 OR to H.F.A.	
	18.		Training under Company arrangements. A bayonet course was constructed for practice in bayonet fighting. 3 OR to H.F.A.	
	19.		D Coy found 1 officer & 50 for a working party. Other companies carried on with training. Under instruction from the bombing officer every man was shown how & threw a MILL'S Bomb. 1 OR to H.F.A.	
	20		Holy Communion was celebrated at 7 a.m. & 8 a.m. & Evening at 6 p.m.	

Army Form C. 2118.

154 Inf: Bde
1/4. L.N. Lanc. Regt.

WAR DIARY
or
INTELLIGENCE SUMMARY.
(Erase heading not required.)

Place	Date	Hour	Summary of Events and Information	Remarks and references to Appendices
	Dec 21.		Notice was received that we should go into the trenches in the afternoon & relieve 1/7 BLACK WATCH in G1A subsector. O.C. Coy.s, Bombing & Intelligence officers with the C.Q.M.S.s arrived in the trenches at 9.30 a.m to take over stores etc. The battalion left BOUZINCOURT by 1/2 coys at 200ᵡ distance at 4.30 p.m. A Coy leading followed by B,D & C coy's. Permission from the Bde was obtained to go by the direct road through AVELUY instead of via ALBERT. The relief was successfully completed at 7.12 p.m. Fire trench:- D. B. A coy's. Right to left. On our right over our left dispositions. C coy was in support. with the 1/6 SCOTTISH RIFLES on our left. the 153 Inf: Bde with the 1/6 H.F.A. 6 O.R.s to H.F.A.	
	22.		During the night 21/22 the wire was thoroughly examined & found to be in a very bad condition. The trenches were	

WAR DIARY
or
INTELLIGENCE SUMMARY.

(Erase heading not required.)

Army Form C. 2118.

1/4 N. Lanc Reg!
15th Inf: Bde.

Place	Date	Hour	Summary of Events and Information	Remarks and references to Appendices
TRENCHES	Dec			
	22.		Very wet & the sides continually falling in. We had plenty of pumps but the water was in fact on it so hurried out. Stiff brooms were found to be very effective in getting rid of the mud & water which was swept down the communication trenches.	
			1 M wounded 4 to H.F.A.	
	23		Nothing of importance to relate	
			4 ORs to H.F.A.	
	24.		Our artillery carried out a fire scheme the main object being to reduce "THE MOUND" which the enemy use for "sniping" & Machine Guns. The scheme was well carried out & did a good deal of damage. The enemy replied but the majority of their shells were "duds" — they were quickly silenced by our artillery.	
			3 OR 4 H.F.A.	

Army Form C. 2118.

1/4 L.N. Lanc Regt
154 Inf. Bde.

WAR DIARY
or
INTELLIGENCE SUMMARY.
(Erase heading not required.)

Place	Date	Hour	Summary of Events and Information	Remarks and references to Appendices
TRENCHES	Nov 25.		The battalion was relieved by 1/4 R. Lanc Regt, moved into Brigade Reserve in AUTHUILLE. Disposition of Companies was the same as on Nov 16th. The relief was successfully completed at 4 p.m. The men had eaten their "tea ration" at midday, & on reaching AUTHUILLE had a good dinner, & the gifts from home were distributed. 2 ORs to H.F.A.	
	26.		No working parties were required & the men spent the day in cleaning etc. 2 OR to H.F.A.	
	27.		125 men required for working parties in fire trench. 2/Lt A. PARKER joined for duty from the Base. 6 ORs to H.F.A.	

Army Form C. 2118.

1/4 L.N. Lanc Regt.
15th Inf. Bde.

WAR DIARY
or
INTELLIGENCE SUMMARY.
(Erase heading not required.)

Place	Date	Hour	Summary of Events and Information	Remarks and references to Appendices
AUTHUILLE	28.		100 men required for working parties. Our artillery carried out a fire scheme commencing at 2.30 p.m. Enemy sent about 10 shells into AUTHUILLE in retaliation. No damage done. 1 OR to M.F.A.	
TRENCHES.	29th		The Battalion was warned to relieve the 1/6 SCOTTISH RIFLES in G.1.B. subsector. Company commanders, intelligence officer and brushing officer went into trenches in the morning to reconnoitre. Companies moved off at 2.30 p.m. in the order A.B.C.D. and the relief was successfully completed by 4.6 p.m. The left of the battalion rested on THIEPVAL AVENUE and the right on LOCH FYNE STREET. The disposition of companies (right to left) was 'C', 'B', 'A', with 'D' in reserve in TOBERMORY STREET. The 1/8 K.L.R. were on our left flank, and the 1/4 KING'S OWN. R.L.R. on our right in G.1.A. 2/L. FAIRCLOUGH joined for duty from the Base. 2. OR. to H.F.A.	

Army Form C. 2118.

WAR DIARY
or
INTELLIGENCE SUMMARY.
(Erase heading not required.)

Instructions regarding War Diaries and Intelligence Summaries are contained in F. S. Regs., Part II. and the Staff Manual respectively. Title pages will be prepared in manuscript.

Place	Date	Hour	Summary of Events and Information	Remarks and references to Appendices
AUTHUILLE TRENCHES	Dec 30		The day was spent in draining the trench, and in working generally. Wiring was done at night. 2 O.R. G H.F.A.	
	31.		With the exception of a bombardment by our artillery, about 1.0 p.m. the day was quiet. The enemy made little retaliation. To H.F.A. nil. 2/Lt BRYCE-SMITH. rejoined for duty from the Base.	

R. Hindle
Lt-Col.
Comm 1/4 L.N.Lans Rgt.

www.ingramcontent.com/pod-product-compliance
Lightning Source LLC
Chambersburg PA
CBHW081438160426
43193CB00013B/2320